BOOK HOUSE
BEASTLY
SCIENCE

REPTILE ROBOTICS

ILLUSTRATED BY
DAVID ANTRAM

WRITTEN BY
JOHN TOWNSEND

Author:

JOHN TOWNSEND worked as a Secondary School teacher before becoming a full time writer of children's books and a writer-in-residence in a primary school tree-house. He specialises in fun, exciting information books for reluctant readers, as well as fast-paced fiction, reading schemes and 'fiction with facts' books. He visits schools around the country to encourage excitement in all aspects of reading and writing. He has recently written 12 plays based on Salariya's *You Wouldn't Want To Be* series that have been uploaded to the company's new website for use in classrooms.

Artist:

DAVID ANTRAM studied at Eastbourne College of Art and then worked in advertising for fifteen years before becoming a full-time artist. He has since illustrated many popular information books for children and young adults, including more than 60 titles in the bestselling *You Wouldn't Want To Be* series.

Editor: **NICK PIERCE**

Published in Great Britain in MMXVIII by
Book House, an imprint of
The Salariya Book Company Ltd
25 Marlborough Place, Brighton BN1 1UB
www.salariya.com
ISBN: 978-1-912233-43-4

$ALARIYA

1 3 5 7 9 8 6 4 2

A CIP catalogue record for this book is available from the British Library.

Printed and bound in China.

Visit our website at **www.salariya.com**

PAPER FROM
SUSTAINABLE
FORESTS

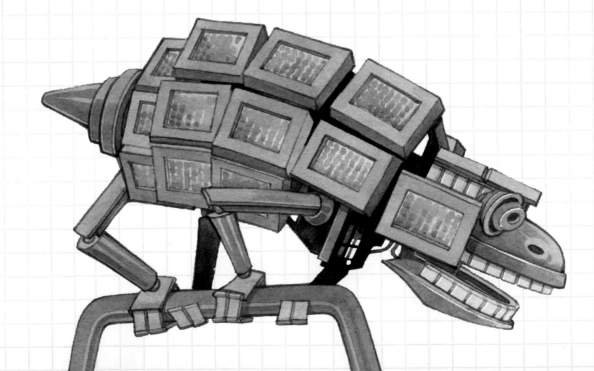

CONTENTS PAGE

ROBO WORLD

Reptiles are changing the world. Many of their secrets are already helping scientists find answers to all kinds of urgent problems.

When scientists and inventors can copy and use animal features it is called 'biomimicry'. It means 'imitating life' and it's Beastly Science at its beastly best. Although reptiles have been on Earth for millions of years, they are now helping to shape the future.

REPTILE REMINDER

Scientists group animals into classes to make it easier to study them. Reptiles are a distinct class as they have dry, scaly skin, breathe air and have backbones. From snakes, lizards and crocodiles to tortoises and terrapins, they all move along either on their belly or on short legs.

Reptiles are cold-blooded so they don't automatically keep a constant body temperature. They must lie in the sun to heat up their bodies. Solar-powered reptile robots do just the same!

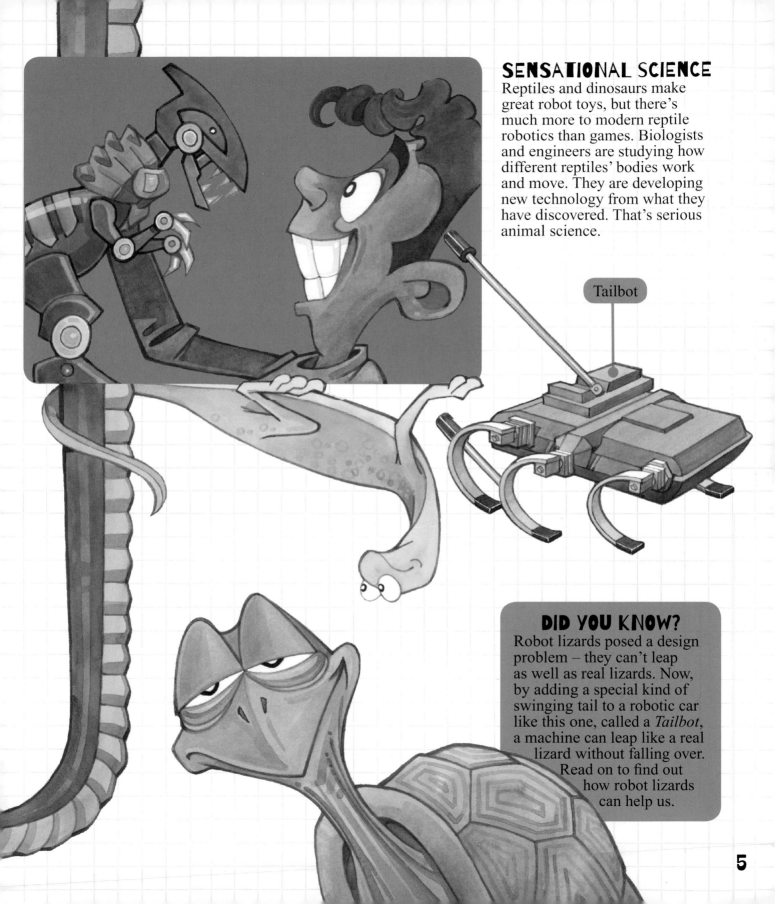

SENSATIONAL SCIENCE

Reptiles and dinosaurs make great robot toys, but there's much more to modern reptile robotics than games. Biologists and engineers are studying how different reptiles' bodies work and move. They are developing new technology from what they have discovered. That's serious animal science.

Tailbot

DID YOU KNOW?

Robot lizards posed a design problem – they can't leap as well as real lizards. Now, by adding a special kind of swinging tail to a robotic car like this one, called a *Tailbot*, a machine can leap like a real lizard without falling over. Read on to find out how robot lizards can help us.

GECKO SCIENCE

A gecko is a type of lizard that lives in warm parts of the world. There are 5,600 species of lizard on the planet and around 1,500 belong to the gecko family. Unlike other lizards, geckos tend to be nocturnal and they make chirping sounds. They also have broad toes covered with flaps of skin containing thousands of bristles. Other lizards have clawed feet.

FACT FILE

- Geckos' feet have special glands (organs in the body that make chemicals) that release and absorb a fine liquid. This substance allows geckos to stick to almost any surface – even polished glass.

- Geckos like to shed their skins. The leopard gecko will shed every two to four weeks. Then (gross alert) a gecko will happily eat the skin it sheds to digest the nutrients it contains. Yum!

- Geckos thrive around humans. In fact, the arrival of a gecko into the home is greeted as a sign of good luck in some places, as it can help get rid of unwelcome insects such as mosquitoes.

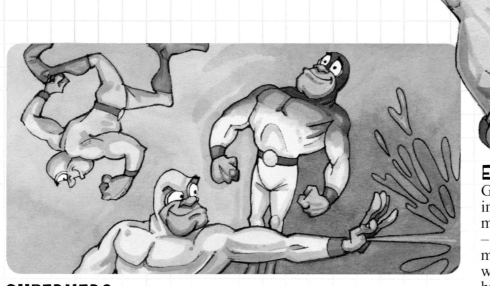

SUPERHERO

Λ gecko has many powers like a superhero's. It can run up walls and across ceilings, lose a body part and re-grow it, change colour or defend itself by shooting sticky goo over its enemy!

ESCAPE ARTIST

Geckos are insectivores. That means they eat bugs – from crickets and moths to mosquitoes and worms. But they are also hunted by bigger predators. When in danger, most geckos can shake off their tails. The discarded tail keeps wriggling and distracts the predator. Meanwhile the gecko escapes, and will often grow a brand new tail.

WHAT A SUCKER!

It's a gecko's skill of running up walls that particularly interests scientists. Millions of tiny hairs and suction pads under a gecko's foot enable it to stick to all surfaces – even slippery steel. What if robots could do the same? Now they can, and so can we!

GECKO ROBOTS

Scientists in California, USA have designed a gecko robot called *Stickybot*. It can climb up the glass walls of a skyscraper. Great news if you want a robot window cleaner!

By studying gecko feet and making fabric to copy all those ridges and bristles, scientists have developed the technology to enable people and machines to scale high walls. *Stickybot* can even change direction mid-climb because it has a rotating foot, just like a gecko's.

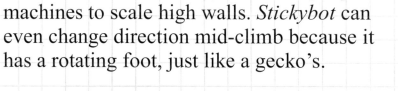

Stickybot

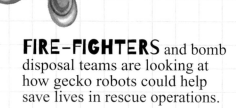

FIRE-FIGHTERS and bomb disposal teams are looking at how gecko robots could help save lives in rescue operations.

GRIPPY BUT NOT STICKY

Materials inspired by the unique physics of gecko fingertips could allow robotic hands to grip nearly any type of object without needing to use pressure. Think of the possibilities...

GECKO GLOVES AND BOOTS

Scientific research continues copying the special way geckos climb. Grippy fabric for gloves, knee-pads and boots have already helped a 70-kg (154 lb) man to scale a glass wall like Spider-Man – or should it be 'Gecko-Man'? Perhaps in the future, if you forget your door key, you will be able to climb up the wall and get in through your window!

9

GECKO EYES

Scientists at NASA are developing robots that can grip objects in space, in the same way a gecko sticks to walls. Such robots could be vital for grabbing onto 'space trash' that could otherwise cause collisions. Scientists have also been looking into gecko eyes. Geckos have excellent eyesight, and they can also see very well in the dark – ideal for hunting at night. The way the lenses in their eyes work has inspired optical engineers developing telescopes, night vision goggles and cameras that film in the dark.

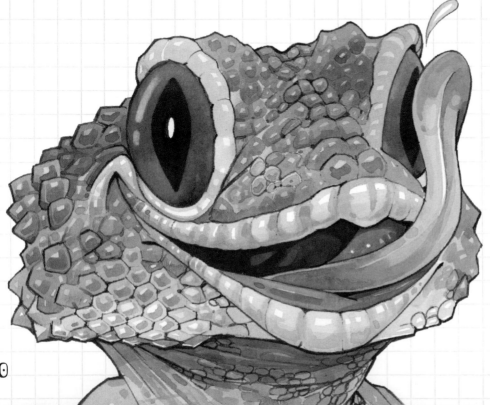

Most geckos can't blink because they don't have eyelids. Like snakes, their bulgy eyeballs are covered with special transparent (see-through) scales that protect the eyes. To keep them clean, some species of gecko use their tongues like windscreen wipers.

To protect their eyes, many geckos have vertical pupils that close to tiny slits to block out damaging sunrays. Some have pupils that close up altogether and they see through tiny pinholes at the edges of the pupil. Their eyes can easily adjust to the brightest light.

Most geckos are nocturnal. They have special light receptors in their eyes which makes them extra sensitive to light. That means they can see really well, and in colour, at night. In low light the human eye only detects shades of grey. Gecko 'eye technology' is now improving human eyesight...

11

NIGHT VISION

I f you go outside at night with a box of crayons and a piece of paper, you'll struggle to work out the colours in your drawing. That's because we aren't good at seeing colours in the dark. A gecko artist wouldn't have this problem!

Geckos have a series of distinct circular zones, like rings, in their eyes that help them see colour at night. This is something very few other creatures have. Would you like to see in the dark just as well as you can see in daylight? With a little help from gecko 'eye science' it might be possible to improve night goggles and cameras.

QUICK REMINDER
A contact lens is a thin plastic film that sits on the surface of the eye to help you see better. Many people wear contact lenses instead of glasses. Multifocal contact lenses based on gecko eyes are already being developed.

DID YOU KNOW?
Something like 125 million people around the world use contact lenses. As far as we know, not a single gecko needs them!

NIGHT VISION GOGGLES help us see in the dark but they're still very clunky compared to a gecko's eyes. One day in the future, glasses or contact lenses that help us to see better at night may result from developments in gecko 'eye science'.

At night, the 'rings' in gecko eyes help them focus sharply on objects at different distances. This allows light of different wavelengths to focus on their retina at the same time. That makes the gecko's night vision 350 times more sensitive than ours. We are colour blind in dim moonlight – but not the gecko.

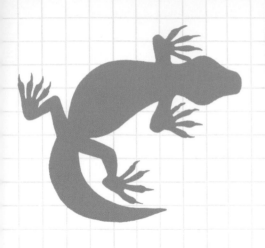

GILA MONSTER SCIENCE

The Gila monster is really a big lizard. It can reach 60cm long and is the largest lizard in the United States, where it lives in the hot, dry desert areas of Arizona, New Mexico, Utah and California. Gila monsters are dark grey and covered with orange, pink, red or yellow spots. They eat smaller animals and reptiles but are very fond of birds' eggs. They thrive in the heat, have thick chunky tails that store energy as fat, and have a very venomous bite! Unlike a snake, the gila monster doesn't inject venom. It clamps its jaws around its victim and gnaws. Venom slowly dribbles down into the bite. Painful as it is, a gila monster's bite isn't usually too dangerous to humans.

FAST FACTS

- Gila (pronounced 'hee-la') monsters can survive for about 87 days without drinking.

- Their name comes from Arizona's Gila River basin, where they were first discovered.

- A group of Gila monsters is called a 'lounge', which makes sense as they lie around soaking up the sun's rays.

- In the wild, a Gila monster can live for 20 years, and possibly up to 30 years in captivity.

A **GILA MONSTER'S VENOM** is as powerful as rattlesnake venom, but the lizard only delivers a small amount of it.

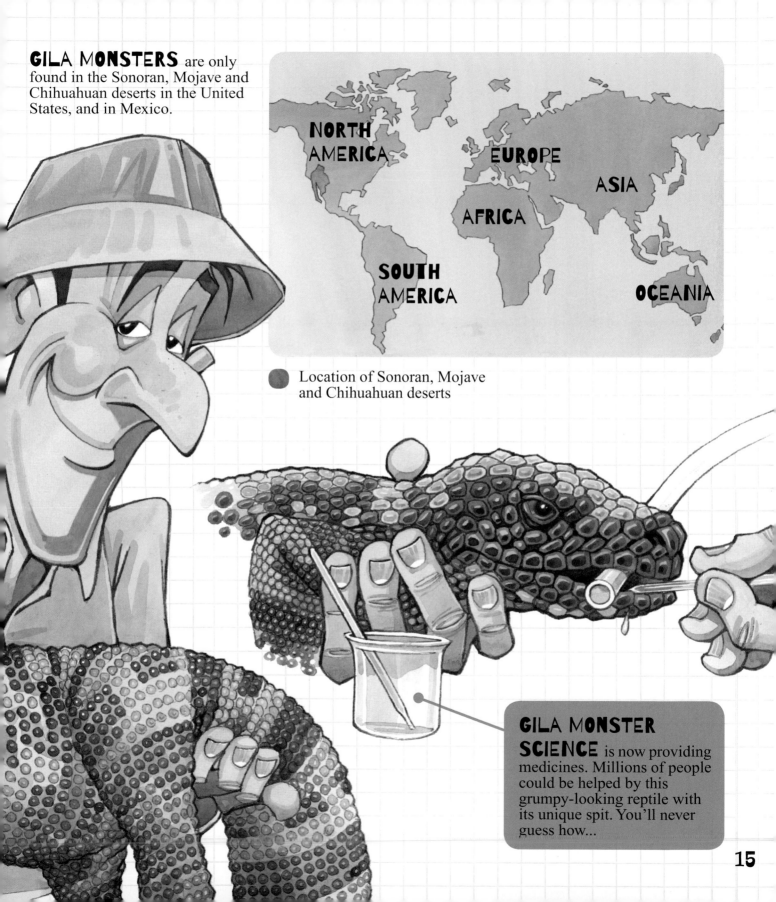

GILA MONSTERS are only found in the Sonoran, Mojave and Chihuahuan deserts in the United States, and in Mexico.

NORTH AMERICA

EUROPE

ASIA

AFRICA

SOUTH AMERICA

OCEANIA

Location of Sonoran, Mojave and Chihuahuan deserts

GILA MONSTER SCIENCE is now providing medicines. Millions of people could be helped by this grumpy-looking reptile with its unique spit. You'll never guess how...

FROM ROBOTICS TO BIOTICS

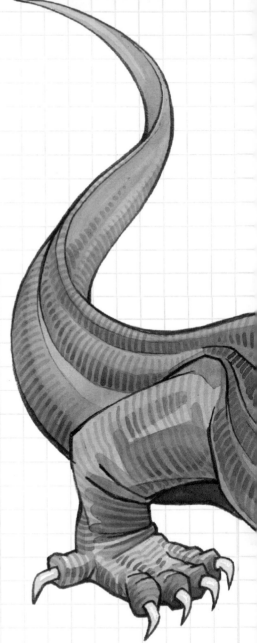

A gila monster robot may be more like science fiction, but gila monster biotics are fact! 'Biotic' means anything living. The gila monster's saliva is being used to treat human disease. Millions of people around the world suffer from diabetes and a special substance found in gila monster venom is being used in drugs to help diabetics regulate their blood sugar levels.

QUICK REMINDER

A diabetic has too much glucose, or sugar, in the blood. Our bodies use sugar for energy. Insulin is a hormone that unlocks that sugar, releasing it from the bloodstream into body cells. If there isn't enough insulin, the sugar levels rise in the blood and diabetes results. Patients have to inject insulin regularly – but drugs developed from the gila monster are already helping some patients.

BIOTICS TO ANTIBIOTICS

Antibiotics can stop harmful organisms and heal diseases or infections. Scientists are studying the blood of reptiles in the hope of developing better antibiotics.

A crocodile's immune system helps it to recover from injuries that would kill other animals. Their blood is being used to help kill superbugs that make people ill.

The Komodo dragon is the largest lizard on the planet. Scientists are studying a chemical in its blood that seems to kill germs and speed up the healing of wounds.

CHAMELEON SCIENCE

A chameleon can see a tasty insect many metres away. It catches prey by waiting for it to come close enough to use its super weapon: its tongue. A chameleon's tongue can grab its prey in just 0.07 seconds – that's faster than a jet plane!

CHAMELEON FACT FILE

- Different species of chameleon range in size from 15 mm (0.59 in) to 69 cm (27 in). That's about the size of a cat!

- Chameleons eat insects like locusts, mantids, grasshoppers, stick bugs and crickets. They drink water droplets on wet leaves.

- Chameleons prefer to be alone. They only hang out with other chameleons during the mating season.

The tip forms a kind of suction cup that is coated with sticky mucus (over 400 times thicker than human saliva). The mucus is like glue, giving the tip of the chameleon's tongue its super grip.

CHAMELEON EYES

Chameleons have super-clever eyes which can rotate and focus separately, so they can see two different objects at the same time. This gives them a full 360-degree field of vision.

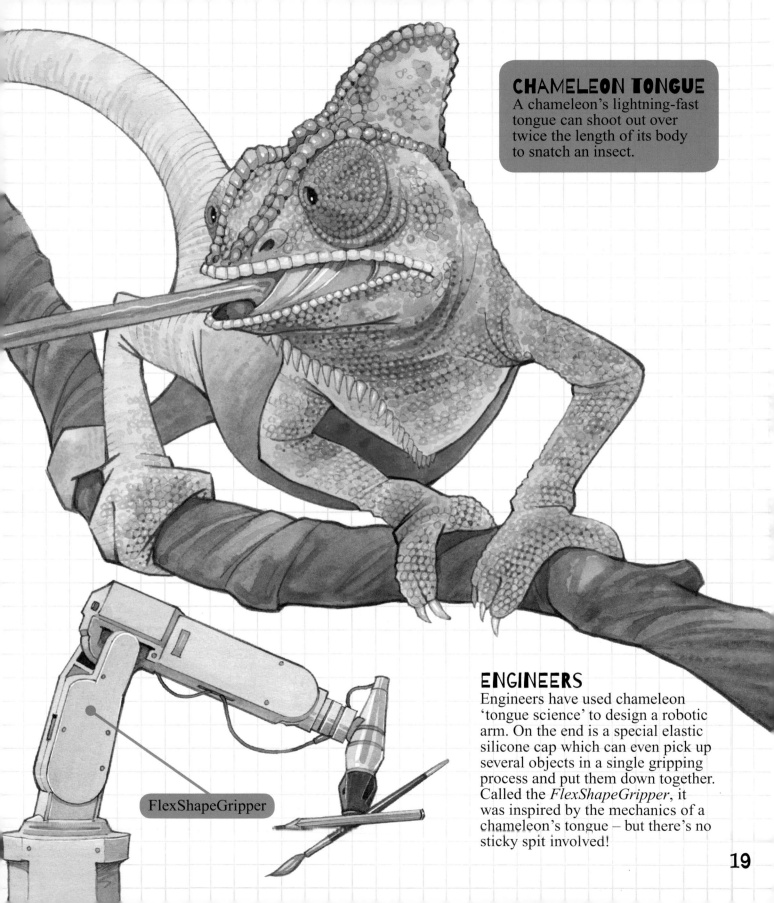

CHAMELEON TONGUE

A chameleon's lightning-fast tongue can shoot out over twice the length of its body to snatch an insect.

FlexShapeGripper

ENGINEERS

Engineers have used chameleon 'tongue science' to design a robotic arm. On the end is a special elastic silicone cap which can even pick up several objects in a single gripping process and put them down together. Called the *FlexShapeGripper*, it was inspired by the mechanics of a chameleon's tongue – but there's no sticky spit involved!

COLOUR SCIENCE

Many chameleons can change their skin colour very fast – but how do they do it? They adjust a layer of special cells in their skin, to change the structure and patterns on the surface. The ability to change colour is used for camouflage and to send messages to rivals. Hanging relaxed on a branch, a chameleon might be green or brown, but when it sees a rival male lizard, it can turn orange and red in an instant. Think of what humans could do if they had the same ability to change colour at will.

IN CASE YOU WERE WONDERING...

Yes, there are chameleon robots. Scientists in China have created 'real-time light manipulation technology' on a robot chameleon. Plates all over the robot change colour like a chameleon's scales. Its 'eyes' scan the colours around it and hey presto, it almost disappears by blending in with the background colour.

If you prefer a bigger colour-changing chameleon robot, this one (right) is at the Robot Zoo at the Children's Discovery Museum in Bangkok.

DESERT CHAMELEONS

become black to absorb heat when it's cool, then light grey to reflect heat. That's super-cool colour science!

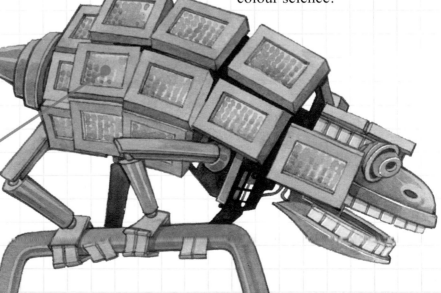

SNAKE SCIENCE

Snakes bring a shudder to many people. Maybe that's because these hunting reptiles slither, wriggle and hiss. But it's some of the horrifying things about snakes that scientists find so interesting. Snake venom contains chemicals not found anywhere else. They can affect the blood and muscles of animals in many ways, so scientists are using venom to develop various medicines.

SNAKE FACT FILE

- About 3,000 different species of snakes are found around the world, apart from Antarctica.

- All snakes are carnivores but only about 600 are venomous.

- Snakes smell with their tongue. They can even sense warm prey in the dark with it.

- Some sea snakes can breathe partially through their skin, allowing for longer dives underwater.

DID YOU KNOW?

Scientists keep discovering new things about snake venom. Some snakes, like the Belcher's sea snake (below), have such strong venom that just a few milligrams of it could kill 1,000 people. Luckily it tends to avoid humans.

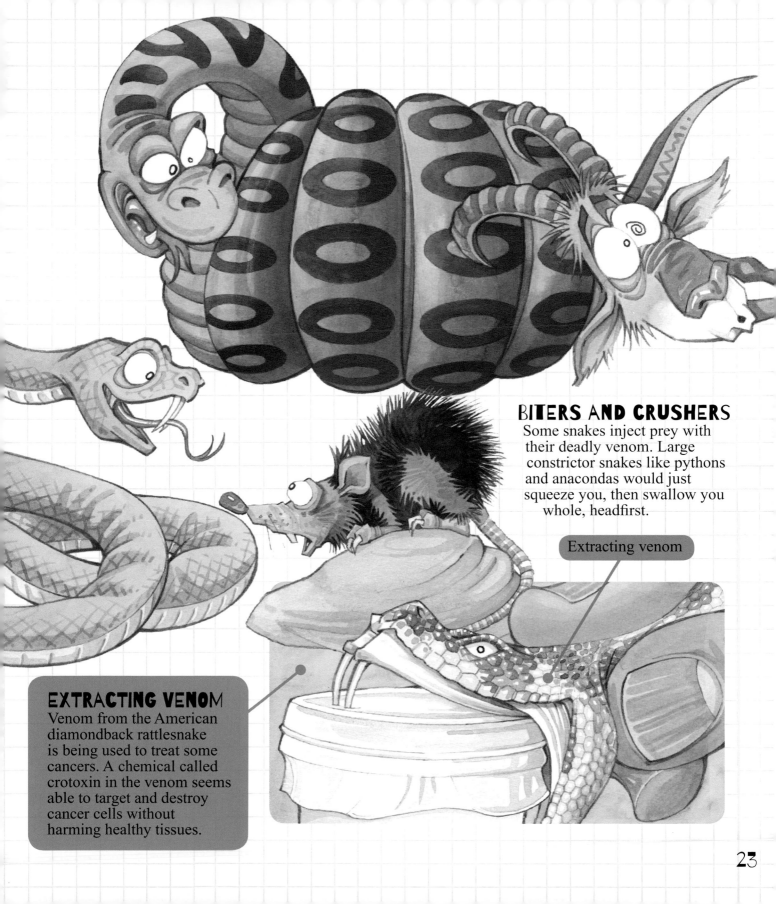

BITERS AND CRUSHERS

Some snakes inject prey with their deadly venom. Large constrictor snakes like pythons and anacondas would just squeeze you, then swallow you whole, headfirst.

Extracting venom

EXTRACTING VENOM

Venom from the American diamondback rattlesnake is being used to treat some cancers. A chemical called crotoxin in the venom seems able to target and destroy cancer cells without harming healthy tissues.

ROBO SNAKE

Snakes are experts at slithering into dangerous or awkward spaces. So scientists have made snake robots that copy how snakes move. They can send these twisting robots to places people can't get to – on Earth or beyond.

Machines aren't very good at moving up slippery and sandy slopes without getting stuck. But sidewinder snakes can. Engineers designed a sidewinder robot with a camera to help archaeologists find out whether parts of ancient Egyptian boats were hidden in dangerously unstable man-made caves by the Red Sea.

THE CARNEGIE MELLON SNAKE robot has mastered slithering up sandy slopes.

JAPANESE COMPANY HIBOT made a snake robot able to move inside air ducts and other narrow places where people can't go.

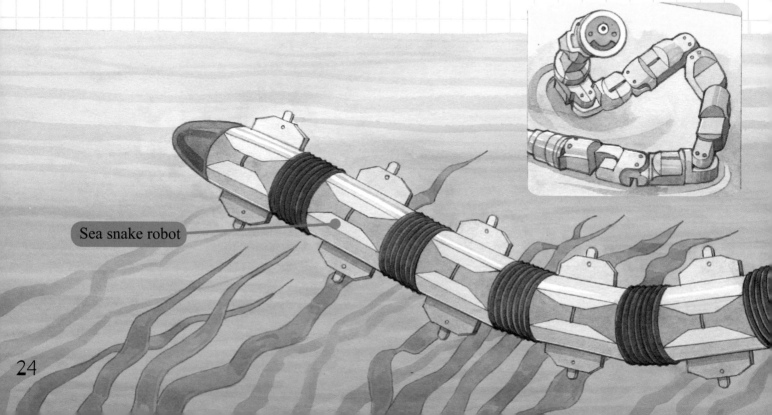

Sea snake robot

24

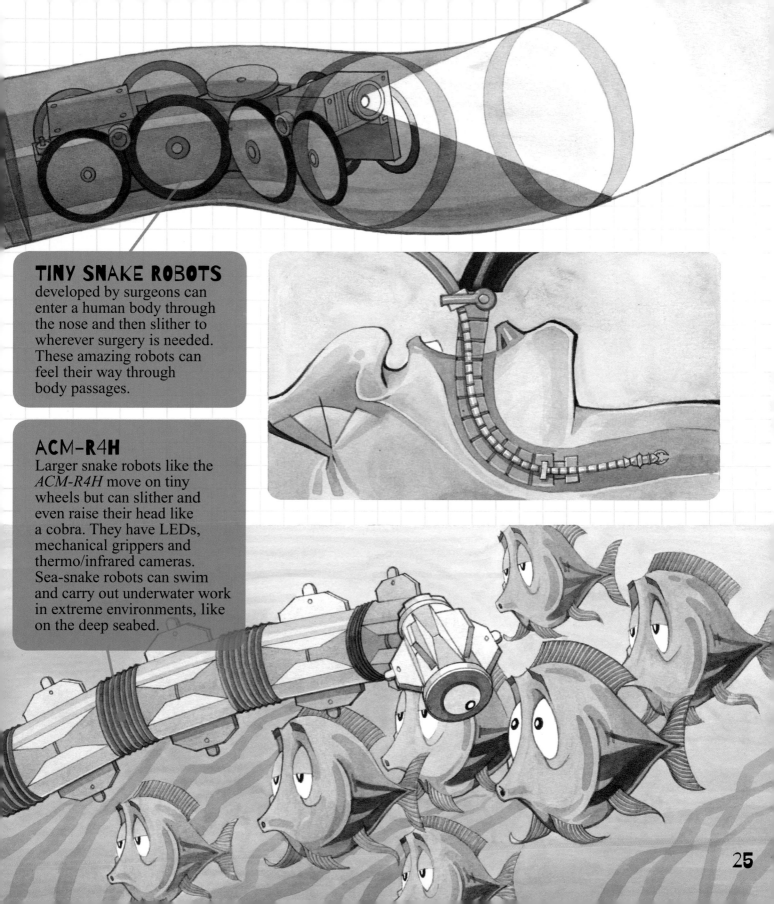

TINY SNAKE ROBOTS

developed by surgeons can enter a human body through the nose and then slither to wherever surgery is needed. These amazing robots can feel their way through body passages.

ACM-R4H

Larger snake robots like the *ACM-R4H* move on tiny wheels but can slither and even raise their head like a cobra. They have LEDs, mechanical grippers and thermo/infrared cameras. Sea-snake robots can swim and carry out underwater work in extreme environments, like on the deep seabed.

25

BASILISK LIZARD SCIENCE

How would you like to run on water? Physics and fancy footwork helps the basilisk lizard to escape from predators. Basilisk lizards can run on water because they have long toes on their rear feet with fringes of skin that spread out in the water. This increases the foot's surface area, acting like a paddle. As they run, they slap their splayed feet hard against the water, making a tiny air pocket that stops them sinking... as long as they keep running fast!

BASILISK LIZARD FACT FILE

- A green basilisk lizard can run 1.5 metres (5 feet) per second on water.

- Green basilisks grow to about 60 cm in length, including their long, whip-like tail. Males have high crests on their heads.

- Green basilisks lay between 10 and 20 eggs. The mothers don't hang around to hatch them. The babies take care of themselves as soon as they're born.

- Green basilisks are omnivores. They eat fruit, plants, insects and small animals.

YOUNGER BASILISK LIZARDS can sprint across the water surface for about 10-20 metres (30-65 ft) without sinking.

GREEN BASILISKS spend most of the time in trees, but always live near water. The rainforests of Central America make an ideal home.

CENTRAL AMERICA

SOUTH AMERICA

Location of the rainforests of Central America.

QUITE A CHALLENGE – Could a robot walk on water like the basilisk lizard? Believe it or not, experts in robotics have been at work designing one…

WALKING ON WATER

nspired by basilisk lizards, scientists have designed a two-legged robot that can move on water, as well as a four-legged version. These have been built and tested – so what next? Smaller water-walking robots that are more like water bugs are now able to scamper over the surface of a pond. This type of robotics is called biomechanics (bio = life).

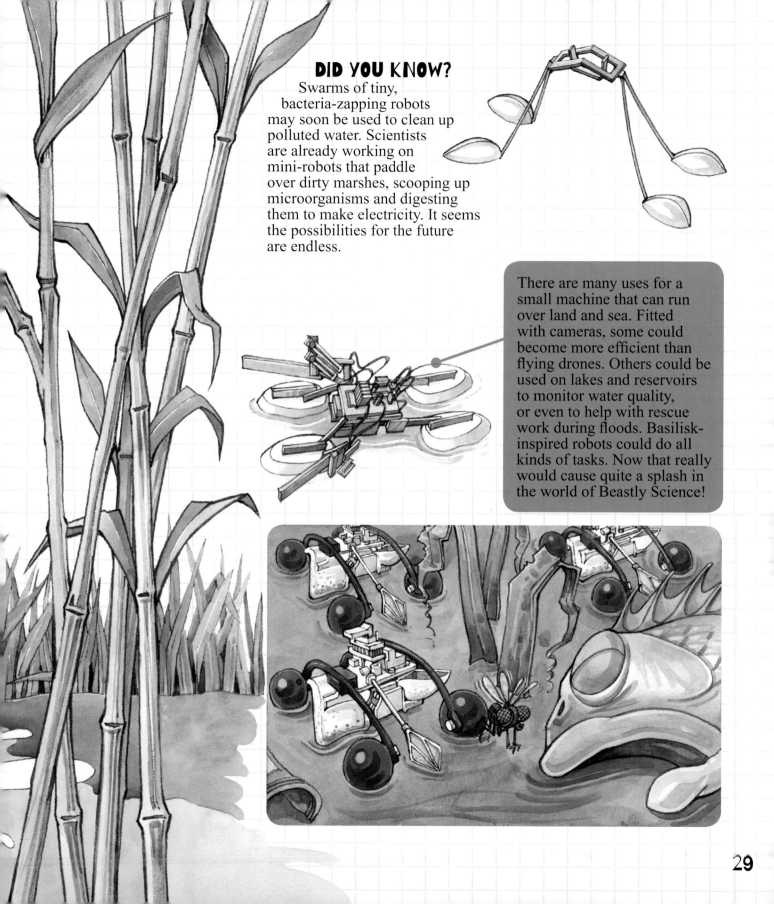

DID YOU KNOW?

Swarms of tiny, bacteria-zapping robots may soon be used to clean up polluted water. Scientists are already working on mini-robots that paddle over dirty marshes, scooping up microorganisms and digesting them to make electricity. It seems the possibilities for the future are endless.

There are many uses for a small machine that can run over land and sea. Fitted with cameras, some could become more efficient than flying drones. Others could be used on lakes and reservoirs to monitor water quality, or even to help with rescue work during floods. Basilisk-inspired robots could do all kinds of tasks. Now that really would cause quite a splash in the world of Beastly Science!

GLOSSARY

Archaeologist a scientist researching past human life from the remains left by ancient peoples.

Bacteria microscopic creatures that can cause disease.

Biologist a scientist who studies living organisms and life processes.

Carnivore a meat-eater.

Constrictor a snake that kills its prey by coiling around and crushing it.

Genes sets of instructions in all our body cells, that make us who we are.

Hormone a chemical produced in a body or plant that encourages growth or affects how cells work.

Mantid insects, usually green in colour, related to grasshoppers and cockroaches.

Microorganism tiny lifeforms such as bacteria that can only be seen with a microscope.

Multifocal having more than one focus.

NASA National Aeronautics and Space Administration (a US organisation which researches space and space travel).

Nocturnal active at night.

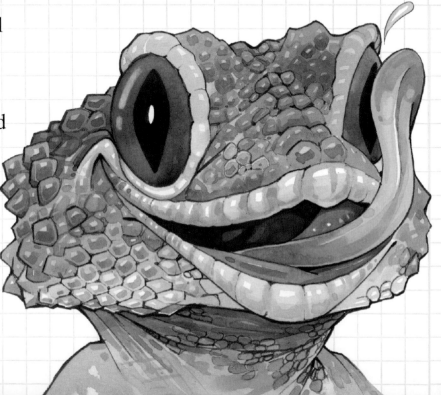

Nutrients substances needed to keep a living thing alive and to help it to grow.

Omnivore an animal or a person that eats both plants and meat.

Optical concerned with eyesight and the relationship between light and sight.

Physics the science of matter and energy and the relationships between them.

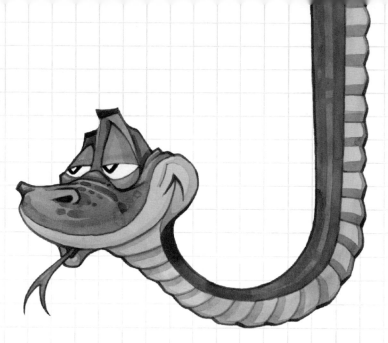

Predator an animal that lives by killing and eating other animals.

Prey an animal hunted or killed by another animal for food.

Pupil the small round black area at the centre of the eye.

Retina a layer at the back of the eye that is sensitive to light and sends signals to the brain about what is seen.

Robotics the science of designing and operating robots.

Saliva liquid produced in the mouth that helps the swallowing of food.

Silicone a mixture of chemicals used to make plastics, water-resistant and heat-resistant lubricants and varnishes.

Solar-powered when energy is produced from sunlight.

Unique the only one of its kind.

Venom poisonous liquid that some animals (e.g. snakes, spiders, fish) produce when they bite or sting.

INDEX